The First 184 Days

ISBNs:
979-8-9935001-4-0 (paperback)
979-8-9935001-5-7 (hardcover)
979-8-9935001-6-4 (eBook)

First Edition, 2025

Independently published by Donatello Dreakford

Cover design by the author.
Interior design by the author.
Edited by the author.

THE FIRST 184 DAYS

Donatello Dreakford

For my Tina.

FOREWORD

I didn't plan on writing another book just yet, this one started as a gift. Tina and I were coming up on six months together, and I wanted to give them something meaningful that documented our story. Something that would last. Not a store bought thing or a quick gesture, but something made from me. Something that could say what words out loud never seem to get quite right.

At first, this was a secret project. I wrote it in hidden moments. While she was at work, or after she fell asleep beside me. I'd wait for the house to go still before I opened my laptop or pulled out my phone, trying to get the words down before they slipped away. It felt like building something sacred in the dark, something small and personal that I could hand to them later and say, *look, this is us.*

I wanted to document those first months together: the little moments, the things that made me laugh, the ways we were figuring each other out. The kind of love that feels like coming home after years of walking in the cold. This book started there. Quietly and privately. It wasn't ever supposed to be published.

At the same time as writing this, I was finishing *Man Enough For Myself*, my first published work. That book came from a different place:

survival, grief, memory, and the work of finally seeing myself clearly. This one came from love. From what happens *after* the self-work and change. From the slow, sometimes awkward, sometimes beautiful work of staying open when you've spent your whole life trying to protect yourself.

For a while, I was writing both books at once. By day, I was editing *Man Enough For Myself*, the hardest thing I'd ever written. By night, I was writing poems meant for one person's eyes. Two kinds of honesty were happening at the same time. One was me talking to the world. The other was me whispering to her.

Three poems overlap between the two collections. I left them here intentionally. When this began, those pieces were part of the original gift, written for her long before I knew this would become its own book. I thought about replacing them, but it didn't feel right. They belong here, in this story. Because this book grew naturally out of that private space. It kept expanding until I realized I wasn't just writing a love letter or private gift, I was creating something that deserved to live beyond us.

I wrote most of this in between work shifts, in the half-light of early mornings or late nights when everything felt still enough to breathe. Sometimes I'd write on my phone in the dark whilst Tina slept. Sometimes in the car before heading into work. I didn't have a clear plan, just a feeling I needed to hold onto and a deadline of our six month anniversary.

Somewhere in the middle of it, I realized I wasn't only writing for Tina anymore. I was writing for anyone who's ever struggled to believe they deserve the kind of love that fulfills. For anyone learning to receive what they once thought they had to earn. For those rebuilding themselves after thinking love was something they'd never get right or deserve.

A big reason I decided to share this book publicly is because people like me, like Tina, *deserve* to be seen. We deserve stories that don't end in tragedy, and a world that doesn't question whether our love belongs here. I wanted to make something that said we exist, that we fall in love, build lives, argue about dinner, laugh until it hurts, and keep choosing each other.

In a time when so many people in charge are trying to erase us, I wanted this book to stand as proof that we are still here, still loving, and still deserving of everything that comes with that.

So yes, this book is for her. It always will be. But if you're holding it now, it's also for you.

For the ones still figuring out what love looks like when it's safe. For those trying to stay open even when it's easier to shut down. For those learning that softness doesn't make you weak, it means you made it.

Thank you for being here, for holding this story in your hands. What started as a secret between two people somehow became my second published work. Thank you for letting me share it.

And thank you, Tina, for inspiring it, for teaching me what patience feels like, for showing me that love doesn't have to hurt to be real. You are the reason this book exists, the reason I look forward to waking up, and making the most of life for as long as I have left on this earth with you.

May,
the beginning.

The start of everything we didn't
know we needed, and everything we
didn't know we were ready for.

Donatello Dreakford

We met at my favorite movie theater, the *Regal Meridian* in downtown Seattle, because of a stupid Hinge profile and a joke about farts. Really. On her profile she said something about wanting the kind of relationship where you could fart in front of each other, and I saw cats in all her photos, so of course I sent her a like. The first thing I ever said to her was, *"Real Farter 4 Real Farter."*

That's how it all started.

Back then I was still healing from top surgery, pretending to be one of those polyamorous or ENM types on the apps because I just wanted to get laid, to feel something in this new body. Then she showed up, the complete curveball I didn't see coming, making every plan I had irrelevant. We still joke about it now, how she saved me from my fuckboy era. When she asked on our first date if I truly wanted something open, I immediately backpedaled and nearly begged her to let me keep her to myself. She still makes fun of me for it, but I know she feels the same way.

What she doesn't know is that I almost didn't go. We hadn't talked for over a week after matching, and when she texted on a whim asking if I wanted to see *Sinners* with her that very night, I said I'd *think about it.* I wasn't feeling it. My body still hurt. I had already seen that movie twice. I didn't feel attractive. I didn't feel ready.

Donatello Dreakford

Then an hour before the movie she texted again, said she was getting ready and on her way, and something in me just shifted. I threw on sweats, a hoodie, and put a durag on my head because my hair looked like shit, then walked there because I didn't want to be the asshole who stood someone up. I told myself, what the hell, it was just a movie.

The second she walked in and smiled, it was over. That kind of warmth isn't something you can fake. She hugged me, and I swear every bit of hesitation left my body. I instantly regretted looking like hell, but by the time she went home, I knew she was the one.

From the start, she made me feel seen in a way that was mildly disorienting. Invigorating and horrifying all at the same time. She's sharp, witty, grounded, too smart for her own good, and has never flinched at my sharpest edges. Any worry I had about her not wanting to be with me because I was the first trans man she'd dated, she crushed with ease. If anything, for the first time it has been me who needs to get with the program. From day one it felt like she knew I was hers too.

Maybe she doesn't know this but meeting her changed how I write. Before her, I was just editing halfway finished poems, stapling random pieces together in hopes of it turning into something useable, and trying to make sense of my feelings through whatever words I could dig up from my notes app with no belief anyone would ever want to read any of it. I had this half-made zine scattered across my bedroom floor when she came over the very first night. She picked it up like it was something sacred, stuck it in her bag whether I permitted it or not, took it home, and actually read it.

A few days later when I saw her again, she handed it back with a note that said:

> D,
> Your words reached me – caressed, shook, and opened me. To have this sort of brilliance means to shine, and I can't wait to see the depths your light reaches. I see you.
> T.

That was the first time I ever felt completely seen. Not just wanted, seen. Maybe even truly desired. All my typos, my messy, broken pages, she saw through them. And she didn't just stay. She leaned closer.

That attempt at a zine went on to become my first published work.

That was May, the start of everything I didn't know I needed.

Donatello Dreakford

Last First Date

We met at my favorite theater.

The one with shaky seats
and screen burned walls,
where I always sit alone
in the same row,
in the same seat,
my church made from flickering light.

I had never let anyone into that sanctuary,
but there she was.

Just a little taller than I imagined,
stepping through the entrance
like she'd always belonged
in my quiet world.

When our eyes met,
my breath caught
like the hush in a theater
before the first note breaks the dark.

She looked at me
with warmth,
and I searched her face
for something wrong.

Some flicker of disinterest,
some subtle wince,

Donatello Dreakford

anything to prove
that I had read this all wrong.

But there was nothing,
only softness.

Only the terrifying miracle
of being wanted
exactly as I am.

We arrived late,
missed the first few minutes.

I lied and said
she hadn't missed much
just to keep her close,
to buy time
to explain everything
she'd ever want to know.

I was grateful for the darkness.

Grateful that the screen
lit her cheekbones
and not my trembling hands.

Even someone like me,
dense,
hesitant,
accustomed to missed signals
could feel her enthusiasm
in the way she leaned in.

The way her body
answered mine.

Her arm slowly curled around mine.
Her head found my shoulder.

I kept my face forward
like I wasn't unraveling
at every gentle touch.

It took me three quarters
of the movie
to take her hand.

Once I did,
I had to count my breaths
just to remember
how to stay alive.

Eight hundred and fifty-six.

That's how many more it took
for the credits to roll,
for her to let go,
and for the world to restart.

I didn't let go
until the usher asked us to leave.

And when I did,
the cold of her absence
hit me like a truth
I had no name for.

Donatello Dreakford

She asked to keep the night going.
I said yes,
of course, yes.

We walked arm-in-arm to her car
and my stomach churned
thinking of my messy room,
a room too real
for someone so incandescent.

(It wasn't clean.
She said it was fine,
I chose to believe her.)

We sat on my floor
cross-legged
playing my favorite icebreaker game
while the hours spun
like warm laundry.

Every question she answered
felt like a key,
a name,
a door,
and I collected them
like sacred artifacts.

If she was going to be
as pivotal to my life
as I already suspected,
then every detail mattered.

The First 184 Days | MAY

I listened
like I was studying scripture,
and I swear
she listened to me
with that same care.

As the night softened
and my nerves gave way
to something quieter,
she crawled into my lap
like a cat.

Graceful,
and certain that space
was made just for her.

Then it was.

Maybe it always had been.

She showed me pictures
of her three cats,
and I held her
like a thing
too precious to scare off.

When she relaxed into me,
melted her head
against my chest,
I almost cried.

Donatello Dreakford

My arms have felt empty
since the moment
she left them.

At almost three in the morning
she said she had to go,
but didn't want to.

Selfishly,
I wanted to keep her
right there forever.

Instead,
I made sure she was awake enough
to drive home safe.

(I let her stay
a few extra minutes,
just long enough
to study the puff of her cheeks
as she leaned into her arms.

To memorize
every flicker
of her resting face.)

I wrapped my jacket around her shoulders
and as I walked her to her car
she reapplied her lip gloss,
like the rest of the night:
not subtle,

not shy,
an invitation written in shimmer.

When we said goodbye
she looked at me
like she was handing me a chance.

This time,
finally,
I took it.

Our lips met.

A spark,
then a fire.

Not some shy brushing,
but a moment
that cracked something open.

As if my body
remembered
what it was made for.

Like all those movies
hadn't been lying after all.

It was brief
but it was real,
and I knew with a clarity
I've never had before
that I was going to fall in love.

Donatello Dreakford

Not maybe,
not someday,
now.

And strangely,
instead of fear
I felt light.

Even if she changes her mind.

Even if this isn't
the beginning
of forever.

Just *knowing*
this kind of love
exists,
that my heart is capable of it,
is enough
to make me hope.

Because I've been on
first dates before,
only three now.

Some lovely,
some painful,
most forgettable.

But this?

This is the first time
I've been *sure*
it won't be the last.

And I will do
whatever it takes
to make this
my last
first
date.

Donatello Dreakford

Asymmetrical

The first day we met
we ended up tangled on the floor of my room,
three weeks post-op.

I was still tender,
stitched up and reshaped,
my chest not yet mine,
not fully.

She pressed against me,
her body curling close
like none of that mattered,
like I was already enough.

I wasn't supposed to
let her lean on my chest,
wasn't supposed to
sleep on my side so soon,
wasn't supposed to
risk the soft places
still healing underneath,
but I did.

Because at that moment,
it felt worth it.

After a while
I noticed it.

Donatello Dreakford

A swelling under the skin,
warm,
puffy,
a little sore.

My body steadily collecting fluid,
making a space
I hadn't planned for.

At the clinic
they ran the ultrasound wand over my chest,
and there it was blinking back at me
from the screen,
a dark pocket,
small but certain
sitting beneath the surface.

A *seroma.*

I watched
as they slid the needle in,
felt the dull pressure
as they dug gently
for the right spot.

Ten ccs of fluid
drawn from my body,
lifted away
and still
it wasn't finished.

The First 184 Days | MAY

A week later
I was back,
but this time
there was no more fluid.

Just a hard knot of scar tissue
setting itself in place,
claiming the space
the seroma left behind.

And overtime
the swelling shrank,
but it never fully disappeared.

That side stayed
just a little different,
just uneven enough
to remind me
that something had happened there.

Now when I touch
that part of my body,
I think about
how love arrived
in the middle of all this.

Before I had the chance
to feel finished.

Before I knew
what this new skin
was supposed to be.

Donatello Dreakford

The seroma is fading,
softening,
disappearing,
day by day.

I can't help but wonder
if love will do the same.

Because the body
takes what it needs,
lets go of the rest,
heals whether we ask it to
or not.

But when my skin
forgets the swelling,
when the scar tissue
shrinks into memory,
I hope it still holds
the shape of that moment.

A mark
and a reminder
that even though I am permanently asymmetrical,
even though things didn't go exactly as planned,
I learned to love
what was left behind.

June,
learning each
other.

Love began to sound less like
promise, more like practice. June
was learning the language of us.

Donatello Dreakford

By the end of May, it wasn't just a maybe anymore. We were seeing each other constantly, learning the sound of each other's mornings and the ways we both go quiet. I learned how she shuts down when she's tired, she learned when I'm overwhelmed, I move things around into little piles. That I'll do anything to make a place feel anchored again.

On May 26th, twelve days after we met, I asked her to be my partner. She said yes. Then she said I love you.

And I froze.

I told her to take it back. I told her she didn't mean it. I panicked because I didn't want to ruin what felt perfect by naming it too soon, but she just smiled and said it again.

After that, I spent weeks pretending I wasn't in love with her. Every time we hung up the phone, I'd say, "Love you too—just kidding, *that doesn't count*," like I could joke my way out of what was already true. But it kept slipping out anyway, smoother each time.

Eventually, I stopped fighting it.

The night I finally said it for real, I didn't plan to. It just came out, the way all honest things do. That same day, I wrote *The Way I Say It* for her, trying to make sense of how love can sound like surrender and safety at the same time.

June was gentle in a way I didn't recognize. She never asked for more than I wanted to give. It was the first time someone was okay with closeness that didn't have to turn into sex. Just being near her was more than I could ever ask for. That scared me more than it should have, how easy it was to let my guard down and not notice until it was already gone.

We spent that month playing every "get to know your partner" card game we could find, staying up too late answering questions we already knew the answers to, just because it felt good to keep learning each other anyway. Other nights, we said nothing at all and let the silence do the talking.

By the end of June, I could tell she was happy by the way she'd say yippee! under her breath. I knew every lyric to *Gnarly* because she wouldn't stop playing *Katseye* in the car, and somehow we both learned the choreography too. My clothes had their own space in her closet, and her car keys meant I could get back "home" to her faster.

That's when I knew. This wasn't just the honeymoon part. This was the real thing, and it wasn't going anywhere.

The Way I Say It

I didn't want to rush it,
not because I don't feel it,
but because you're precious to me.

Your heart is something
I never want to mishandle,
and sure
maybe I've been protecting mine too,
but mostly
I've been thinking about yours.

About how people talk,
how people watch
how someone like me
might look like too much
to the ones who love you,
especially after what the last one put you
through.

I don't ever want to be someone
you have to defend,
I want to be someone
you never have to explain.

I've thought I was in love before
but it always came
with shrinking,
with second-guessing,

Donatello Dreakford

with becoming a version of myself
that was easier for someone else to hold.

But you?
You don't ask me to be easier,
you just hold me.

I didn't realize how much I needed that
until I caught myself relaxing
in the hidden moments
I never used to notice.

You scrub my back in the shower
like it's the most natural thing in the world.

You lotion me after,
laugh when I flinch
like I'm not still stunned
by how gently you love.

You keep my toothbrush ready,
keep me in routine
without pressure,
you make the rest of life feel easier too.

When we're apart,
I don't know how I went so long
without this kind of care.

I love cooking for you.
I love driving you places
even when I complain about the traffic.

The First 184 Days | JUNE

I love when you pack my lunches,
and sew little red hearts
into my clothes when they rip.

Your care shows up
in all the places people call small,
but nothing is small with you.

And yes,
I know
I haven't said the words yet.

Not out loud.

But I do love you.
Of course I do.
How could I not?

You make it feel easy to.

I feel it in the mornings
when your face is soft and puffy from sleep,
and you look so peaceful
I could cry just from being near you.

I feel it when my clothes smell like your house,
and I'm reminded I have somewhere
to come back to.

I feel it in every one of your freckles,
I count them in my head
like I'm trying to memorize the sky.

Donatello Dreakford

You've heard the words
even if I haven't spoken them.

You hear it
in the way I stay,
in the way I listen,
in how I reach for you without thinking,
in how I remember the things you say
even when you think I'm not paying attention.

I always am,
because it's you.

There's nothing temporary about this,
no act,
no performance.

Just me,
here,
trying to learn how to be loved like this,
and doing everything I can
to give it back
the way you deserve.

And when I do finally say it,
truly say it,
you won't be surprised.

You'll just smile
like you've known the whole time.

The First 184 Days | JUNE

Because I've been saying it
in the way I hold you,
in the way I come home to you,
in the way I've been writing it
across every ordinary day
we've made sacred
just by doing them together.

Donatello Dreakford

The Quiet Parts

I learned you in pieces
before I learned you whole.

Not through grand gestures
but through the pauses,
the small
quiet things
you probably never noticed.

The way your breathing changes
when you're falling asleep,
how you hum when you're anxious,
the half-smile you make before you say
something honest.

How you look away
right before you say I love you,
like the words might burn too bright
if you watch them land.

You don't know this,
but I time my breathing with yours sometimes,
to feel closer without saying a word.

I trace the shape of your voice in my head
so I don't forget it when you're not around.

You talk to yourself while getting ready,
low and steady,

Donatello Dreakford

and I listen from the other room like it's a song
meant only for the walls.

You stretch when you're thinking,
tilt your head up when you're trying not to cry,
and every sigh you let out
feels like a modest kind of trust,
the kind you only give to someone
who won't ask for more than you can give.

I used to think devotion had to be loud,
to announce itself,
to prove it was honest.

Now it's in these moments
I feel it most,
the mundane routines,
the knowing,
the way your body melts when you're safe.

And somewhere in all that silence,
I started weakening too.

My shoulders unlearned the weight they carried,
my body stopped bracing for goodbye.
You taught me that safety could be steady,
that devotion could whisper and still be heard.

You don't have to say anything.
I already know.

The First 184 Days | JUNE

Because the truth is,
I learned to love you
in silence first.

And in silence,
I still do.

Donatello Dreakford

July,
falling deeper.

Love isn't proven by the easy days.

Donatello Dreakford

You wanted closeness. The kind that feels easy and certain, the kind that comes without hesitation. I wanted distance. Not because I didn't love you, but because my body still equates solitude with security. Touch doesn't always feel simple to me. Sometimes it feels like reopening a door I spent years learning how to close.

You came from a relationship that had gone silent. Six years of trying to be acknowledged, to be wanted, to be held. You were used to promises that never came through, to affection that had to be begged for. I was used to the opposite. People who took from me, people who never asked what I wanted. You were still trying to believe that wanting more wouldn't make you too much. I was still trying to believe that saying no wouldn't make me unlovable.

That night, those histories clashed. You'd reached for me, and I froze. You felt rejected, and I felt ashamed. It was small, but it felt enormous, like our own pasts and the weight of other people's mistakes started speaking through us.

When you went quiet, I panicked. I spent half the night writing, trying to explain that I love you, that I'm trying, that my affection doesn't disappear when my body pulls away. I was terrified that you'd take my boundaries as proof I didn't want you. I just didn't know how to tell you that every time I forced myself past my own comfort, I started losing the very security I needed to stay.

I drove you to the airport the next morning with that same fear lodged in my throat. I told myself you'd be fine, that a week apart might make things lighter. Instead, a few nights later, you called.

Your voice was shaking. You said you didn't feel desired. That maybe we weren't meant to be. I'd never felt that kind of panic before, the kind where love itself feels like it's slipping through your hands and you can't hold it tight enough to stop it.

I realized in that moment that I'd been loving you the way I knew how: careful, quiet, from a distance, instead of loving you the way you needed. You needed warmth. More reassurance. Physical connection that said *I'm here* and *I want you,* and I had been waiting for safety to feel natural before giving it.

That phone call wrecked me, but it woke me up. To how easy it is to think love is enough just because you feel it. To how love means nothing if it isn't fully reaching the person it's meant for.

When you came home, we sat in that new honesty. You told me you were working on unlearning the shame around wanting things like affection, closeness, reassurance, that you'd spent years apologizing for needing. And I promised to unlearn my instinct to disappear when things got hard.

That was the moment I knew we were serious. Not just new, not just shiny. *Real.* Because we faced the version of each other that wasn't pretty, and we stayed.

July was our first make-or-break moment, and we chose to make it.

Donatello Dreakford

Before the Airport

You wanted to hold me,
and I wanted to want that too,
but something in me
was too tired,
too loud,
too full of old ghosts.

I kept trying to explain
that it wasn't you,
that sometimes my body still flinches
at the thought of being wanted,
that I've spent so many years
saying yes
just to survive,
that I don't always know how to mean it.

You thought I was pulling away,
I was trying to stay whole.

The night before you left,
you packed your suitcase
while I packed my words,
trying to make them palatable enough
not to scare you,
yet strong enough
to protect me.

Donatello Dreakford

I told you I love you.
That I am trying.
That every *no*
is me choosing to keep showing up tomorrow.

You went quiet.
The kind of hush that hurts
because it sounds like goodbye.

And still,
I meant every word.

I wasn't saying no to you,
I was saying yes to myself,
so I can keep saying yes to you.

Call from
Virginia

Your voice was shaken that night,
a little cracked around the edges.

You said you'd been thinking
that maybe I didn't want you,
that maybe we weren't meant to be.

The word *meant* felt like a bruise.

I didn't know how to tell you
that I'd been thinking too
about how easily silence
can sound like indifference,
how connection can start to look one-sided
when you can't touch it.

I wanted to say,
I do want you,
I always have.

I just never learned how to show it
the way you need me to.

That sometimes
I mistake stillness for safety,
and forget that love also needs movement.

Donatello Dreakford

So instead,
I sat on the curb outside of my job
staring at the phone light,
listening to you breathe between words.

That's when I realized
this wasn't about blame.

It was about learning
how to meet in the middle,
without losing ourselves along the way.

You said,
"I'm going to work on emotionally
reconditioning myself,"
and I laughed through the ache,
because only you could make healing
sound like a syllabus.

Then you said you were trying to stop
apologizing
for having needs at all.

That's when it hit me,
I had been doing the same thing in reverse.

Apologizing for needing space,
protecting myself from closeness
instead of letting it protect me.

The First 184 Days | JULY

It wasn't an argument anymore,
it was a map,
a way back to each other.

After we hung up,
I sat there for a long time,
thinking about all the ways I'd learned
to love from fear.

How to anticipate,
to provide,
to prove,
but not always to listen.

You taught me that night
that care isn't about doing the most,
It's about doing what matters.

About learning the language
of the person beside you,
and speaking it
even when it's not fluent yet.

I learned that
wanting to be loved
and knowing how to receive it
are two different things,
so are loving
and loving in a way that can be felt.

Donatello Dreakford

That night in July
you taught me both,
and I've been practicing ever since.

*We didn't lose each other that
month. We just stopped assuming
love was enough without
understanding.*

August,
weathering
things.

August was honest.
It asked if we could still choose
each other when it wasn't all new.

Donatello Dreakford

August felt like an exhale. For the first time, everything felt steady, like we had finally made it through the part where love must prove itself.

She'd planned my birthday weekend down to the smallest detail, and it was the first time in my life anyone had gone through that kind of effort for me. I drove us to a little cabin she'd booked in Snoqualmie Falls, tucked beside a river and a horse farm. We spent the night in solitude, letting the sound of the water do the talking for us. The jacuzzi steamed under the cold air while we laughed about nothing. We let the day stretch long without needing to fill it.

That night, she'd found us this hidden mom-and-pop Italian restaurant. Fresh pasta, homemade garlic bread, the kind of food that makes you forget to talk because everything tastes like home. We ended with tiramisu, my first time trying it (and loving it,) and I remember thinking, *this is what it feels like to be cared for without having to earn it.*

The next morning we went to Twede's Café, the diner used in the filming of David Lynch's *Twin Peaks*. It's one of my favorite shows, and sitting across from her there made it feel like a scene I never thought I'd live. She smiled at me over coffee and chicken fried steak like she already knew that.

Donatello Dreakford

When we got back home, she had more surprises waiting. A red velvet cake, a box set of my favorite manga comics, and a fancy massager that still can't compete with the ones she gives me herself. She even managed to somehow print photos from the trip without me noticing, and slipped them into a card, handwritten and perfect. I've never received that much care all at once. It was intentional, and it was love.

I don't usually celebrate my birthday. It's never been something that felt worth celebrating. But that weekend, she made me feel like I'd actually deserved one.

August also brought change. It was the month I *fully* moved in, or at least admitted that I hadn't been to my own apartment for long enough to where it still counted as my residence. It was the month we learned how to share a space without losing ourselves in it. I used to think having someone around would suffocate me, that I'd fold under the weight of being seen all the time. Instead, it's been the opposite. Having her near has been healing and wonderful in ways I didn't think possible.

We started learning the rhythm of us, how to communicate before the tension builds, how to let silence mean rest, and not resentment. She stopped reaching for me to make sure I was still there, and I stopped counting the ways I could disappear.

August taught me what love looks like when it stays. It was gratitude, it was intention, and it was home.

Donatello Dreakford

Twenty-Six

For most of my life,
birthdays felt like paperwork,
another year signed off
without ceremony.

I'd buy my own dinner,
pretend not to notice the silence,
convince myself it didn't matter.

Continuing on never felt
like something to celebrate.

Then there was you.

You planned everything:
a cabin hidden away in Snoqualmie,
the sound of the river flowing a few feet away,
a jacuzzi steaming against the mountain cold.

We were tucked between trees and stillness,
and for once I didn't feel the need to run.

That night we found a small Italian restaurant
with no need for perfection,
fresh pasta,
garlic bread that cracked in our hands,
tiramisu so velvety
it made me close my eyes.

Donatello Dreakford

You kept smiling across the table
like you were memorizing the sight of me,
content.

I'd never been looked at that way before,
as though someone was grateful
I was still here.

The next morning we drove to *Twede's Café*,
the diner featured in *Twin Peaks*.
I used to watch that series to escape,
to live somewhere calmer,
somewhere people like me could just exist.

Now I was there,
sitting across from you,
existing in real time.

When we came home,
you still weren't done.

Red velvet cake.
A box set of my favorite comics.
A handheld massager that could never compete
with you.

Photos from the trip
already printed and slipped into a card
that said everything without saying it outright.

No one had ever made my life
feel worth documenting before.

The First 184 Days | AUGUST

I don't think you know
what that meant to me,
how I've spent birthdays
counting down years I didn't think I'd live on,
how each one felt like a debt I couldn't repay.

Then you arrived
and turned it into a gift instead.

That weekend
I stopped keeping score,
I stopped flinching at the sound
of my own name,
I stopped pretending I didn't want to be known.

Twenty-six wasn't a milestone.
It was a miracle.
It was the first time being on this earth
felt like something I had earned.

And somewhere between the river
and the red velvet,
between the laughter
and the silence,
I started to imagine a future.

One that looked a lot like this.

Ordinary and serene,
the two of us in the middle of it,
building something worth growing older for.

Donatello Dreakford

How We Listen

We used to speak like we were waiting
to be proven right.

Now,
we speak to be understood.

There's no scoreboard anymore,
no sharp edge hiding under the ease.

We talk slower.
We ask before assuming.
We listen even when it's uncomfortable.

I've learned that love
doesn't live in apologies
or in who reaches for who first.

It lives in the moments we pause,
when one of us sighs,
when the air shifts,
when silence starts to sound like a question,
and the other answers with presence.

You have this way of hearing me
even when I don't say anything at all.

You can read it in the way
I set down a cup,
or how long I stand in the kitchen
before sitting down.

Donatello Dreakford

You listen with your eyes first,
your hands second,
your words last.

And I listen to you
the way I wish someone had listened to me,
without fixing,
without defense,
just the steady hum
of knowing you're safe.

Sometimes it's not even about the conversation.

It's about what comes after,
the laughter,
the subtle return to touch,
the simple fact that nothing was lost
in translation.

Living together taught us
that love is maintenance.

Not grand,
not fragile,
not loud,
maintenance.

The muted kind
that needs showing up,
the daily work of hearing
and being heard.

This is how we listen now,
not to win,
not to prove,
to continue.

Donatello Dreakford

September,
roots.

September was where love became
familiar, and familiarity became
something sacred.

Donatello Dreakford

By September, things had started to take shape. The pace slowed down, and what was left between us was something sustainable. I began to see how love changes once you stop chasing the high of newness. What we had was more faint now, but it held. It had weight.

She and I slipped into a rhythm that didn't need much discussion. She packed my lunches before work, and I made sure her gas tank was never empty. We went grocery shopping together while arguing over snacks and brands, which type of apple was best, ending every trip with something we didn't need but couldn't leave behind. I always ended up conceding, and we moved through those aisles like a small team: efficient, bickering, always snickering together by the end.

Cohabitation was something I used to dread. I thought it would feel like shrinking, like I'd lose the little autonomy I'd fought to build. With her, it was the opposite. Living together didn't erase me like I thought it would. It gave me more room to exist. She didn't take up space, she expanded it. I started to realize that love could be reliable without being dull, that sharing a life didn't have to mean disappearing inside it.

Fall came fast, and with it came the kind of heaviness that tends to follow both of us when the light fades. We've always had that in common, the

Donatello Dreakford

way sadness and depression can creep in unnoticed until it's sitting with us in the room like another roommate. But it's different with her. When one of us starts to fall behind, the other fills the gaps. If she slips, I steady her. When I stop caring for myself, she's already handing me my medication before I can talk myself out of it. That's the thing about this kind of love, it's not about rescuing. It's about keeping track. It's about observing, and understanding.

It shows up in the smallest things. Her folding my clothes when I forget them in the dryer. The toothbrush with paste she put on it waiting by the sink in direct sight before bed. The way she sleeps on the couch when I'm gone, just so she's the first thing I see when I get home from a night shift. They're tiny gestures, but together they show a map of what we've made. Something lived in, something whole.

By the end of September, I registered that we weren't just trying to keep the spark alive anymore. We were tending to something else entirely, the daily, elusive work of choosing each other. That's what love had become for us: not the rush, but the return.

Our partnership wasn't smaller now, it had simply embedded. And for the first time, I didn't feel trapped in routine, I felt rooted in it.

Beginnings

She bought the house before I was here,
a slim gray new build
stacked like a spine,
two bedrooms and a half bath
that doesn't quite count.

It was one of those modern places
that looked expensive
but felt hollow,
too clean to hold a life.

When I moved in,
it wasn't ours yet.
It was a box waiting to be lived in,
waiting for color,
waiting for noise.

Now the fridge is covered in our handwriting,
a grocery list beside the whiteboard of reminders,
love notes and poems
layered like a collage of two people
trying to make sense of joy.

The cats own every surface,
their hair,
her hair,
mine.

Donatello Dreakford

Her favorite yellow blanket on the couch,
the crocheted quilt she made
to cover the ottoman stain
we keep promising to replace.

The dying plants by the windows
I swore I'd care for.

Matching electric toothbrushes
that whirr in sync.

We live on the *megacouch*,
a Frankenstein of furniture
big enough for two people
and three cats to sprawl across
like it's the only piece of earth that matters.

Some nights,
we don't even make it to bed,
we just sleep wherever we land,
limbs tangled,
television humming low.

Our days fall into steady familiar patterns.

She starts puzzles she never finishes,
and over time
the cats scatter the pieces like confetti.

Evenings are spent with her lesson plans
spread across her lap,
me editing drafts beside her.

The First 184 Days | SEPTEMBER

We pause to talk,
to eat,
to listen to each other's exhaustion,
her stories about the kids she teaches,
mine about the patients I care for.

It's our kind of stillness,
two lives emptied out
refilled by the other's voice.

Sometimes we read in silence,
or play card games,
or just exist in the same quiet
that used to scare me before I met her.

Now it feels like proof
that comfort
doesn't have to mean distance.

The stairs are never clean,
cat hair clings to every step
and I sweep them anyway.

We shower in the hallway bathroom
because the tub in the master still leaks,
and neither of us has called anyone to fix it.

The house is imperfect,
but it's alive.

It hums with us.

Donatello Dreakford

She built this place on her own,
and I think about that often,
how much strength it takes
to make something alone
and then open it up
for someone else to enter.

I didn't build these walls,
but she lets me fill them,
my books,
my mess,
my writing,
our noise.

We talk about marriage sometimes,
about the kind of life we want,
a quieter town,
three kids,
a wraparound porch,
a cat farm in the yard.

We joke about how boring we are,
how traditional our dreams sound
for two queer people,
how somehow that feels radical.

We talk about saving enough
so she can stay home when we start our family,
how I want to buy her a ring
when it's the right time,

how I'm scared the world might try
to take those dreams away from us.

This isn't the house we'll grow old in,
but it's where the idea began.

Where color started seeping into gray,
where the ordinary became evidence,
where we learned that home
isn't the place itself,
it's the way we fill it,
the way we plan for what's next
even before it exists.

It's just us and the cats for now,
but sometimes,
when the house is quiet,
I can already hear the future
walking up the stairs.

Donatello Dreakford

October,
looking back and
preparing
forward.

October was reflection. It was the realization that we built something that we both want to last.

Donatello Dreakford

By October, our love had stopped feeling like something fragile. It became something we could lean against. There were still the occasional disagreements, moments of irritation, unwashed dishes, and half-finished conversations, but none of it ever lasted. The tension always melted by nightfall, the way light softens at the end of the day. We had finally reached that place where loving someone wasn't about avoiding the mess, it was about trusting that we'd find our way through it together.

It's strange to think how much has changed since May, back then I thought love had to feel like falling. Like chaos, like ache. I thought stability meant boredom, and steadiness meant settling. I didn't know it could be this: laughter while folding laundry, shared glances across the grocery aisle, delicate apologies whispered over takeout. I didn't know love could be a language spoken subtly but felt everywhere.

You and I built this from nothing. From an app, a movie date, a half-hearted swipe that somehow rewired my life. Every month since has felt like a different version of learning. Learning to listen, to speak, to stay, to see each other fully. We've gone from curiosity to comfort, comfort to commitment, and somewhere in between those things I found the version of myself I had been trying to grow into all along.

Donatello Dreakford

October feels like a pause between chapters. We're still in the middle of it, but I can already see what comes next. We've made plans, real ones, not just daydreams said to fill silence. I'm meeting your family. You're coming across the country to meet mine. That's something I never thought I'd do. I've spent most of my life keeping people at a distance, guarding the truth of who I hold dearly. You changed that.

Sometimes I catch myself watching you when you're not paying attention. The way you move through the world with ease, how your mind works ten steps ahead, how your warmth makes even the coldest rooms feel like they belong to us. You're independent, capable, everything I admire, yet still let me care for you in all the small ways that matter. You've taught me that strength and softness don't cancel each other out, that love can be both giving and being given to.

And you've learned me too. The shortness in my voice when I'm tired. The stillness I slip into when I don't know how to explain what's wrong. You don't take it personally anymore. You meet me where I am, sometimes with patience, sometimes with a well-deserved call-out. You've shown me that love doesn't need to tiptoe around flaws, it just needs to understand them.

This month, I see all the ways we've grown. How every stage of our story has layered into something solid. You've built me up in ways I didn't think were possible. I've started reaching for better because of you. Better jobs, better words, better days. You've made me want to stay alive and keep evolving. You've taught me to look for the color in things again.

Six months is not forever. But I think of all that has happened between the first message and now, and it already feels like a lifetime. The nerves, the lessons, the tenderness, the fights, the laughter. Every version of us lives somewhere inside this one.

October feels like standing in the doorway of everything we've built. The life behind us still warm, the one ahead just beginning to take shape. It's where I look at what we've made and think: this is what it means to love, truly. Not because it's perfect, but because it's ours.

Donatello Dreakford

184 Days

Day one,
the Regal.

Me in sweats and a durag,
you in a smile I didn't know I'd remember.
I almost didn't go.

You hugged me and something inside me
stopped hiding.

For the first time in a long time,
I didn't feel like a mistake in my own skin.

By day twelve
I'd already asked you to be mine.

You said yes
and I love you
in the same breath.

I panicked, told you to take it back,
and you refused.

Weeks later,
it slipped out of me by accident
and you only smiled,
like you'd been waiting for my heart
to catch up to my mouth.

Donatello Dreakford

Around day thirty,
you started leaving things at my place.

A hair tie,
a hoodie,
a corner of your toothbrush beside mine.

You learned my silence,
I learned your rhythm.

Love still felt new then,
soft,
uncertain,
like walking barefoot
into something warm.

By day sixty,
we stumbled.

You wanted closeness I didn't know how to give.

I pulled away,
you pulled harder,
the space between us filled with
misunderstanding.

That night I wrote you a message,
and you chose to listen
instead of leave.

We learned how to argue
like people who wanted to make it.

The First 184 Days | OCTOBER

Day ninety was water and air,
Snoqualmie Falls,
steam curling from the hot tub,
the sound of the river outside our cabin
singing over everything else.

It was my twenty-sixth birthday,
pasta,
garlic bread,
tiramisu.

The first one that felt like celebration
instead of getting by.

By day one hundred twenty-six,
we were living together.

A tall gray house,
cat hair on every stair.

Your yellow blanket on the couch,
our grocery list on the fridge,
love notes layered over receipts.

We learned that care
could look like chores,
and routine could feel like devotion.

Around day one hundred fifty,
the quiet stopped being something to fill.

Donatello Dreakford

We worked side by side,
you with your lesson plans,
me with my dreams and words.

Evenings spent half-talking,
half-existing.

By day one hundred seventy,
the future stopped feeling theoretical.

We said *when*
instead of *if.*

We made plans,
the kind that stretch past next week.

You told me about your family,
and I started thinking about mine.

About names for children,
about the porch we'll sit on one day,
about the way we'll age into each other.

And now,
day one hundred eighty-four.

Half a year since the night I almost stayed home.
Half a year of slow growth.

I've learned that love
doesn't always make itself known.

The First 184 Days | OCTOBER

Sometimes it grows quietly,
through mornings that blur into evenings,
through ordinary acts that mean everything.

You've taught me that care is not performance,
that strength doesn't mean solitude.

You've made me softer,
more deliberate,
more here.

You've given me a reason to look forward
without bracing for loss.

It's been one hundred and eighty-four days
of building something real,
and if I could count them all again,
I wouldn't change a single one.

Because that fondness didn't happen
in a moment.

It happened every day after,
in the choosing,
in the returning,
in the quiet rhythm of two people
still learning what forever feels like.

Donatello Dreakford

Now They See

At first,
it was too new for anyone to believe in.

People smiled,
said we looked good together,
then waited for the shine to fade.

They'd seen me fall fast before,
burn out just as quickly.

They didn't understand
that this time wasn't fire,
it was foundation.

Days stacked into weeks,
weeks into months,
and what we built
started to speak for itself.

Your name in my routines,
mine in yours.

The small things told the story,
the groceries bought in pairs,
the car we share,
the way your toothbrush lives beside mine,
how our plans stretch past next month
without either of us flinching.

Time has a way of testing things.

Donatello Dreakford

People stopped asking
if we were still together.

They started saying
you instead of she,
us instead of me.

I think that's how love announces itself,
not through declarations,
but through grammar changing
around your name.

Now they see the life we've made
faintly holding itself up.

The dinners,
the trivial arguments that never last,
the simple joy that always returns.

The house full of books and warmth,
the proof that comfort can still be alive.

We didn't rush to convince anyone,
we just kept showing up,
day after day,
until our union stopped being new
and started being known.

Sometimes I think about all the times
I tried to prove my worth to people
who couldn't see me clearly.

How easy it would've been
to shrink again,
to hide the good thing
just to keep it safe.

But this time,
I let it be visible.

I let *us* be visible,
and the world didn't fall apart,
it adjusted.

Now they see what I've known
since that first night at the Regal,
that actual love doesn't need defending.

It doesn't have to be loud
to last.

It grows slowly,
quietly,
without permission,
until one day you look up
and grasp everyone else
has finally caught up
to the truth you've been living in.

And maybe that's the point,
not to prove anyone wrong,
but to keep loving each other long enough
for time to take your side.

Donatello Dreakford

What's Next?
Our Future.

The future looks like mornings
beside you. It looks like the next
184 days, and the next, and the
next.

Donatello Dreakford

Currently everything feels suspended between endings and beginnings. The air outside has that late autumn stillness, and the house smells like chai, cat fur, and unfinished projects. You keep asking what I'm writing, and I keep pretending it's nothing. You pout when I won't let you read it, but I think deep down you already know.

This book is for you. It always has been.

It's hard to explain what it feels like, trying to build something new while the rest of my life still feels uncertain. I'm in between jobs, watching the clock on rent, counting what's left in my account, wondering if anyone will read the first book I ever wrote that comes out in a few days, wondering if they'll read this one too. I'm terrified most days of failing, of falling short, of not becoming the man I keep trying to be. But even through that fear, I know you'll be there, building me back up, hyping me up like you always do. You'll call me brilliant before I believe it, and you'll mean it even if nobody else does.

Next month, I'll meet your family for the first time. The idea makes my stomach turn in every direction at once: excitement, nerves, hope, the miniscule wish to be accepted. I've been practicing Vietnamese phrases under my breath, rehearsing them in the mirror like a performance I can't mess up. I wonder if they'll notice my nervous hands, or the way my voice shakes when I talk too long.

Donatello Dreakford

I wonder if they'll see me for who I am, and not what I used to be. But when I picture you there beside me, I stop worrying about being deserving. You've never asked me to prove I belong, you've just made space for me too.

Soon after, you'll meet my family. That part feels lighter, like something that's been waiting to happen. I've never brought anyone home before. Never said, *this is who I love*. Never wanted to, until now. You'll meet them during the holidays, and I think they'll finally understand what I mean when I say I'm happy.

Sometimes, when I think about what comes next, it doesn't even feel like a dream anymore. It feels like a map, sketched but genuine. A house with a wraparound porch and a swing that creaks. Three kids with names we already know. A few more cats running underfoot. A kitchen filled with noise and morning light. You teaching our children what gentleness looks like, me trying to keep up.

We talk about marriage, about someday being older, slower, and still here. You at twenty-seven, me at twenty-eight. I want to save enough to buy you a ring that shines but still feels like us. I want to buy a car that's mine, contribute to your mortgage, and stop living like everything could fall apart at any second. I want to be steady enough to give you the kind of life you deserve. I want you to rest.

We laugh sometimes about how traditional we sound, the trans man who wants to make enough for his wife to stay home, the nonbinary partner who says I make them feel like a girl again. We both grew up craving simplicity, I think. Not quiet in the sense of smallness, but the kind that means stable.

Before all that, we want to see the world. Maybe New York City, maybe somewhere in Europe. Maybe Vietnam, where you'll show me where your family came from. I want to taste the food, hear the language roll off your tongue, watch you come alive in the place that built you.

And maybe someday, we'll come back to Washington. Somewhere green, slow, and quiet. The house with the wraparound porch we keep talking about. A place to raise our family, to grow old, to hold what we've built.

I don't know what life will look like by then. Maybe I'll be an author, and people other than you will read these words someday. Maybe I'll finally go to school for mortuary science, and I'll end up in another funeral home, not answering phones this time but working with my hands, restoring what's been lost. Maybe I'll still be writing for just your eyes. Maybe I'll do all of it.

Donatello Dreakford

Wherever I end up, I want to look over and see you there, your yellow blanket, your puzzles, your half-finished tea, your glasses falling down your nose and your laughter.

You've made me believe in the long version of things. You've turned tomorrow into something I want to reach for.

The future doesn't scare me anymore. It looks like mornings beside you. It looks like all the days still to come.

Two Letters From T.

Donatello Dreakford

*In the beginning, it was her
handwriting. Her voice, steady and
certain, building a world we hadn't
stepped into yet.*

May 20th, 2025

I'm at work watching students take a test. My forehead is sticky with sweat and my eyes are strained from darting my watchtower gaze back and forth.

The fluorescent lights make the blue screens of the Chromebooks shine harsher, and yet, all I can think about is you.

The softness of your eyes when they linger on my lips. The way your breath catches when those same lips meet your neck. Your fingertips caressing every crevice and curve that ache for your touch.

Though this electrified attraction sends a current through me, one that reminds me how easily my body can yearn, they are becoming periphery to the visions of what a life together would look like.

We'd live in a pale yellow, one-story home (I'm DONE with sweeping cat hair built up step by step). It'd have a wraparound porch that creaks a little when we shuffle out on it to drink our morning tea, the noise amplified due to how quiet our little rural sanctuary is. The breeze would pick up the tail ends of your scarf and flit in my face from how close I stand to you.

- T

Donatello Dreakford

May 21st, 2025

We would sit on the metal blue chairs we scored from a town fundraiser auction for retired race horses, our seats cushioned by covers I made from old quilts. Our ritual would begin — cups down, books open, free hand resting on yours. I'd be able to tell when you've read a particularly riveting part by the way the grip of your hold changes. This is how we would spend our slow mornings, amongst the gerbera daisies and snapdragons (both cat-friendly flowers of course).

The calm of our morning would be broken by the faint soft mews of hungry bellies, woken from the soft stream of sunlight that gleamed in from the bar's stained glass windows. They're not really stained glass — just a peel and stick we found at Walmart, but we had fun putting it up. We'd look up from our reading with knowing eyes and get up from our seats hand in hand to stroll towards our little ones we love so dearly.

But, for right now, I'm full of contentment with what we have. And I have to proctor this test.

- T

Wraparound Porch

You dreamed it first,
the pale yellow house,
the creak in the porch boards,
the breeze that caught your scarf
and brushed my face.

You wrote about mornings
that sounded like contentment,
about chipped mugs cooling in our hands,
cats threading through the garden,
and how that contentment could live
inside ordinary hours.

I didn't know it then,
but you were writing us into being.

Now we live in something smaller,
grayer,
built upward instead of wide,
a house that bustles with our noise.

The air purifier's low hum,
the cats,
your voice
floating through rooms
that never stay clean for long.

We haven't reached the countryside yet,
but we've found what you described.

Donatello Dreakford

The house changes with us.

Each week something new appears,
a shelf,
a bruise,
a laugh line,
proof that we're learning to take up space here.

The light hits different
in rooms we've made our own,
like the house is finally changing with us.

Our love moves through the day in patterns:
keys tossed on the counter,
shoes by the door facing opposite directions,
a half-finished cup of coffee beside the laptop,
your voice calling me back to the present.

It's not the things we keep,
it's the life we make between them.

You start puzzles when your mind needs calm,
I write when mine refuses it.

Somehow,
both are little acts of returning.

We don't need to explain each other anymore,
you move through the house
and I know what kind of day it's been
by the way the door closes.

The First 184 Days | OUR FUTURE

The future isn't waiting on us,
it's already under our feet.

Every floorboard remembers
the weight of choosing.

You once said you could tell
how much I was feeling
by the way my hand held yours.

Now my hand doesn't shake.
Now I hold back less.

The future you dreamed
doesn't live on paper anymore.

It's here,
in the undertone between our breathing,
in the light that waits for us to wake,
in the small proof that we've arrived
without even noticing.

We're not on that porch yet,
but every day feels like a step toward it,
another nail driven,
another beam set.

Love builds itself slowly
in quiet persistence,
until one morning you look around
and understand you've already made it.

Donatello Dreakford

One day we'll sit where you imagined,
tea in hand,
the porch creaking beneath us,
the breeze moving the air between our breaths,
our children shouting from the yard.

And I'll know it started here
in this narrow gray house,
in this acquiescent,
imperfect season,
in these one hundred and eighty-four days
that turned a dream
into a life.

To my Tina.

For all the things we haven't done yet, but will together.

Yours,
Donatello

About The Author

Donatello Dreakford is a Black trans author, artist, and aspiring mortician currently based in Washington. His literary work explores love, identity, and the small rituals that make a life feel whole. He is a former performer shaped by the drag and ballroom communities, and he writes with the same truth and tenderness that once guided him on stage.

The First 184 Days is his second self-published collection, a portrait of love in real time, of learning, healing, and choosing. When he's not writing, Donatello spends his days with his partner Tina and their three cats, finding joy in quiet moments and the life they're building together.